Published by
Lion Publishing plc
Sandy Lane West, Oxford, England
ISBN 0 7459 3362 9
Albatross Books Pty Ltd
PO Box 320, Sutherland, NSW 2232, Australia
ISBN 0 7324 1324 9 ·

First edition 1995
10 9 8 7 6 5 4 3 2 1 0

The Lord is my Shepherd

Words of comfort from the Bible

illustrated by Linda Smith

LION
Giftlines

Linda Smith's 'leaves and petals' collages follow the seasons from autumn, through winter and on to spring and summer. They echo the Psalmist's journey from sorrow to hope. The traditional symbolism connected with many trees and flowers is given here as an aid to meditation. Linda's sensitive work adds an extra dimension to the Psalm and its message.

Elm: *dignity and deep-rooted faith*
Poplar: *courage*
Maple: *quiet peace*
Chrysanthemum: *truth and love*
Willow: *mourning*
Yew: *sorrow*
Holly: *suffering – Christ's crown of thorns*
Ivy: *faithfulness*
Mistletoe: *'I surmount difficulties.'*
Fruit blossoms: *a sign of hope*
Almond: *God's approval*
Peach: *silence and a virtuous heart*
Cherry: *sweetness of character and good works*
Primrose: *sadness*
Bluebell: *constancy*
Snowdrop: *hope*
Oak: *faith*
Hawthorn: *hope*
Roses: *time and eternity, love and death*
Sweet pea: *parting*
Rosemary: *remembrance*
Forget-me-not: *true love*

Introduction

*T*here are moments in life when words fail us, when there is nothing we can say that will express our feelings and thoughts. Bereavement is one of those times.

Yet there is one poem, surely one of the best known and loved in the world, that seems to bring comfort and help in a unique way: the Shepherd Psalm from the Old Testament of the Bible.

It is short. Its ideas are simple and direct. It springs from a culture and a time far removed from our own. Yet it breathes a real sense of the presence and love of the Shepherd himself.

This beautiful book is designed around this timeless Psalm, in the hope that it will bring to you its message of comfort and love.

The Lord

is my shepherd,

I shall

not want.

ULMAC

He makes me

lie down

in green pastures;

he leads me beside

still waters;

he restores my soul.

He leads me

in right paths

for his

name's sake.

Even though

I walk through

the darkest valley,

I fear no evil;

for you are with me;

your rod and

your staff —

they comfort me.

ILEX AQUIFOLIUM

You prepare

a table before me

in the presence

of my enemies;

You anoint

my head with oil;

my cup overflows.

LILIACEAE

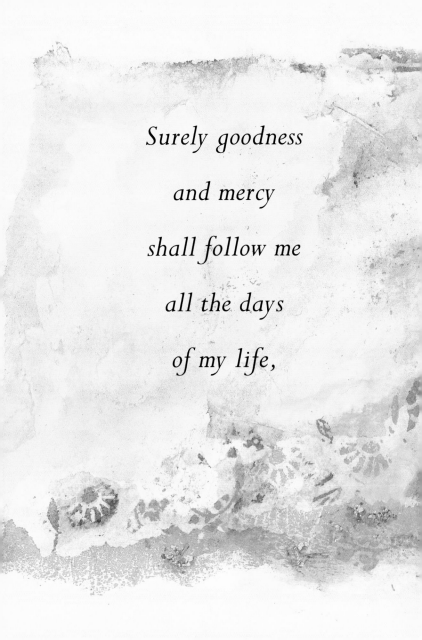

Surely goodness

and mercy

shall follow me

all the days

of my life,

QUERUS ROBUS

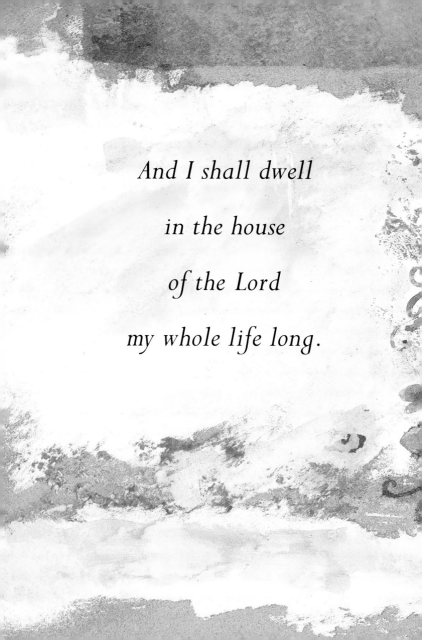

And I shall dwell

in the house

of the Lord

my whole life long.

Thoughts
and
Prayers

Out of the depths I cry to you,

O Lord;

O Lord, hear my voice.

FROM PSALM 130

But now, this is what the Lord says –

he who created you. . .

he who formed you. . .

'Fear not, for I have redeemed you

I have summoned you by name;

you are mine.

When you pass through the waters,

I will be with you;

and when you pass through the rivers,

they will not sweep over you. . .

I am making a way in the desert

and streams in the wasteland.'

FROM THE BOOK OF ISAIAH

Through

the

valley

of

the

shadow

of

death

Goodness

and

mercy

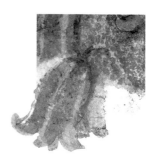

*J*esus said, 'I am the
resurrection and the life.
Whoever believes in me will
live, even though he dies; and
whoever lives and believes in me
will never die.'

FROM THE GOSPEL OF JOHN

*W*e give back to you, O God, those whom you gave to us. You did not lose them when you gave them to us and we do not lose them by their return to you. Your dear Son has taught us that life is eternal and love cannot die, so death is only an horizon and an horizon is only the limit of our sight. Open our eyes to see more clearly and draw us close to you that we may know that we are nearer to our loved ones, who are with you. You have told us that you are preparing a place for us; prepare us also for that happy place, that where you are we may also be always, O dear Lord of life and death.

WILLIAM PENN

In the house of the Lord, for ever

*T*his I call to mind and
therefore I have hope;
Because of the Lord's great love
we are not consumed,
for his compassions
never fail.
They are new every morning;
great is your faithfulness.

FROM THE BOOK OF LAMENTATIONS

Set me as a seal upon thine heart,
as a seal upon thine arm:
for love is strong as death.

FROM THE SONG OF SONGS

*G*od's promise of
resurrection is written
not only in books
but in every springtime leaf.

MARTIN LUTHER